Poetry The 21

Eight Years of Wonders

Anikunj kanojiya

BookLeaf Publishing

India | USA | UK

Made with ❤ on the BookLeaf Publishing Platform
www.bookleafpub.in
www.bookleafpub.com

Dedication

To those who find comfort while reading poems and
enjoying every single sentence of it which make them
believe in everything that they want to achieve.
The more you read the more you know love.

Preface

This book is the collection of different types poems, some are is divided into parts. Some are romantic, some are thrilling, some are joyful and many more.
Poetry The 21 Eight Years of Wisdom as the name suggests
Book content 21 poems by the author, which are his great creations in these eight years (2018-2025) and that where the subtitle came from "Eight Years of Wisdom."
These poems, the more you read the more you know love.

Acknowledgements

I would like to express my sincere gratitude to Bookleaf Publishing for giving me this great opportunity and to my cousin sisters who support me and inform me about this Great platform. I'm really grateful to my family members for supporting me and all my friends. thank you for reading and loving my poems.

.

Lastly I would like to express my gratitude to all the readers.
Thank you for loving my poems, your love for poems make them lively and give me more motivation for keep writing.
Thank you from my heart.
Dear readers, the more you read, the more you know love.

Maa and Papa thank you and love you.

Song of Death Chapter 1

A small flower bloom on the white thick snow,
I remember watching her how well she grow,
It was a warm winter when me and her first met,
I don't know it's good or bad just take a deep breath,
She smile at me with tears of love in her eyes,
Loneliness melting me, with my heart open wide.

I had a dark past, that define me as an illusion,
I created a hell to destroy, my love of emotions.
I ask everyday why me and her met,
When I already starts writing, my own Song of Death.

A small bird flew away in a big scary sky,
I was happy outside but inside it's a lie.
I keep going down and follow her till the end,
I remember everything except the time we together
spend.

I dream about dying, I dream about life,
I dream about killing her, with the hate made of knifes.

Why I keep following her after knowing I'm going to
regret
When I'm in the middle of singing, my own Song of
Death.

I burn the flames of love to hate her like hell,
To protect her from myself I become a hatred shell.
We saw each other and laugh for a while,
She told me "don't worry I'm at your side"
I want someone to rewind the time for me,
I want to know her and I want to see.
I want to give a reply when she smile at me.
I want one more chance to have more regret,
I want to stop singing, my own Song of Death.

My Stars Are Aligning To You Part 1

I saw you shining under the blue summer sky,
To see your smile my heart tells a sweet lie,
Waves from the ocean start playing the rhythm,
We both are dancing in the field of our own sins,
My eyes are tearing for the blissful time we share,
Missing each other even though we both are here,
I take your hand and my heartbeat run fast
Even if it is a dream, I hope it will forever last.

When The Moon starts Glowing again and again
When my love for you become more and more insane
When Flowers start singing the hymn of love for you
Every moment become magical, Do you feel it too
Even if it is the end or the beginning of something new
It's the sign God is saying, My Stars are Aligning to you.

Dream of Reality

Oh It's a dream, Dream of reality,
In which I'm imprisoned to the time of eternity,
It always showing me what I wanted to keep,
Stuck up in my head, like a disturbed visuality,
Why I'm here when I'm not supposed to be,
No it's a dream, Dream to Reality.

Wooh it's a bird, different at least it's free,
Blooming with the sky opposing the reality,
Fly above high, fly as far as you can,
Escape from this fake dream,
where life can be different.

Wake me up already, I've sleep enough,
Free me from this hell, it's already tough.
One day your wings will be blue and grey,
I hope you and me just fly far away,
I hope you always have a reason to stay,
You always will be my dream from yesterday.

The Demon From Hell 1 : Diablos

In the middle of the night,
Walking on the shore,
The sea was silent,
That wasn't like before,
I heard someone whispering,
Through my ears to my core.
Said "I came from far away to take over you"
My body was shivering, through and though.
I turn back and see that someone was there
Smiling big, and his eyes had that glare,
My soul was ripped , like he was having fun,
Start counting backwards three, two, one,
Snap his fingers and just say it ones,
"I'm Diablos,The King of Demons"

Fireflies

Alone in the dark, when no light will able to find me,
Moon is no where to be found like it's been hiding,
Darkness taking over, and the silence is climbing,
I'm standing here and saw something shining,
Why would I ever be Worried,
Fireflies will guide me.

Taking me away, leading the way,
Twinkling like the stars, lighting the dark,
Embracing lights, shining on every mark.
Everything is already decided for me,
Why would I ever be Worried,
Fireflies will guide me.

Singing With Your Rhythm

Birds are chippering, woods Start singing,
It's their own rhythm of life, that they are giving,
Wind around here is a musical instrument,
Poetry is dancing taking away the moment,
Under the spotlight that is rain by the stars,
I stand there and watching, but not too far.

I feels it on my lips, when the beat hits the drum,
Making a way for me, the stage is set in their kingdom,
My legs start moving and lips syncing when it comes,
Now I'm High on music and Singing With Your Rhythm.

Feel the nature's music that began to shaken up the core,
Everything starts shining, when the king of the jungle
roars,
I keep drowning in here where life takes a new form,
Sometimes summer becomes colder, and winter is warm,
My soul enters a eternal realm and piece hit my mind,
When they dance to the fullest, dancing becomes their
design.

Forgetting all the worries, I'm just waiting again for my
Turn
When I'm just dancing and singing in the prime of their
kingdom
It's the spirit of the, jungle that makes me here summon,
I'm just High on music and Singing With Your Rhythm.

The Demon From Hell 2 : Averruncus

He was Laughing out loud as I was trembling from fear,
He starts walking towards me and I watch him coming
near,
The Moonlight Embracing him, as the drakness he wear,
The Supreme Monarch of Demons, Lord Diablos is here.

Sky was getting Red like he spread Blood all over,
Wind is getting cold, as he comes closer and closer.
He took my hands and look into my eyes,
My legs were freeze, like I'm being paralysed.

"I'll be taking your soul", he said to me,
"You belong to my world, The next Lord Supreme",
He saw the aura I possess was stronger than his.
The will to destroy and the will to live.

I saw myself Sitting on the throne of the King,
All demons were hailing, there heads are down bowing,

"You'll be the destroyer, the Strongest among us",
"Long live our Prince of death, Lord Averruncus".

The Demon From Hell 3 : Rise of The Lord

I'll Reign Over You, through your flesh and soul,
I'll be immortal, Underworld will be in my control,
Moon and Stars will follow my rules, my command,
They'll witness my wrath, End of this world will be
grand.

March my Demons, its time for you to show,
Lord Averruncus is here, whole world should Know,
It felt like my emotions were gone, all humanity was
lost,
I'm left with hunger for power, no matter what is the
cost.

Diablos is with me, Calamity is in our hands,
Destruction everywhere, doesn't matter who stands.
Begone or take my hand and become one of us,
Bow down your heads and hail Averruncus.
Accept Your fate, you won't survive
In the end the Dark Lord will Rise.

Umbrella : In Rain and Thunder

Oh my dear Umbrella, The rain is still going,
My heart is still floating through the water it's pouring,
Wind is getting colder and sundenly stop blowing,
It's safe under you but I'm always afraid of Loosing,
Oh my dear Umbrella, the rain is still going.

Something made me afraid, what it was I wonder ?
I looked up at the Cloudy Sky, It was the Raor Of
Thunder.
Above My head someone dancing and playing drums,
Sky is looking flashy when the thunder and rain comes.

Flew away from my hand, in the Storm so far away,
Don't leave me behind in the night blue and grey.
I'm still searching for you in the storm that soaring,
Oh my dear Umbrella, The rain is still Going.

Song of Death Chapter 2

Hello to the illusions that stuck up in my mind,
Forging the memories of her, making them unwind,
Dethrone my love and singing the blues of wonders
Asking me again, "will you regret or make me surrender"
I wish to see the end that he will write for me and her
I want to see the sky beyond that one bloom flower.

A boy who fell in love will be lost in the realm of depth,
To see her smile again and the promise that we long
kept,
It's written all over again on my body and breath,
I'll meet her again, I'll again sing the Song of Death.

I'm counting the endless arrows that coming towards me,
Ready to Pierce my heart into countless peaces,
They are giving me scars all over again and again,
My eyes are just into you, doesn't even know the pain.

Do you remember the time when You and I first met,
Warm winter was it ?

Now the summer sun is going to set,
Even if the rain is pouring I'll sing without any regret,
Rewinding the time to the moment where our eyes met,
Even if I am incomplete will you always accept ?
To the last thrill of my life I'm always ready protect,
With Roses in my hand, I'll sing the Song of Death.

My Stars Are Aligning To You Part 2

Summer rain, I'm dancing in style with you,
Winter again, snowflakes showering upon you.
Sorry I'm running late to catch up with the time,
Everlasting moments, for the perfect you and I.

Our story of today, will become the legend of tomorrow
The path I chose, is the path of pain and sorrow.
Wonderful isn't it, my love for you is blooming again
Echoes around are saying, you and I are always one
frame.

I'm seeing visions, parallel dimensions are in my head,
Which one is of you ? I'm afraid the ending will be sad.
The darkness I see suddenly looks colorful with you,
I'm singing my hearts delight, now I've found my cue.

When the night meet its end, I'll be waiting at your lane,
When the Sun starts showering, its golden shine again,
You become the sunshine, that guide me out of vain.

When I become the drying summer, you'll be my Rain.

When stars align they rewrite fate,
A boy a girl, are heavens made,
We found the love that couldn't fake,
When the moonlit sky was unaware in night,
We're the ones shining under its light.
When I'm in the sea of lies, to me only you seems to be
true,
Even if you're at the Horizon, you know I'll Make it
through,
Just look at the sky and see, My Stars Are Aligning To
You.

The Demon From Hell 4 : Abyss Lost Soul

Once a demon who always smile,
In the depth of darkness where he resides,
Looking down on humans having a despise,
Souls were his soldiers, walking dead were his knights,
Just the eco of "Hail Averruncus" was left and right.

Ashes were everywhere flying with the wind of joy
It's his mind that creates and his hands that destroy.
It's the fate he choose that made him disappear
His soul was lost in the Abyss of death and Fear.
The one shall punished for the sins he wear
Mocked by the Gods as his end comes near.

He seeks revenge and perform the sorcery
Reincarnated his soul as human with lost memories.
He curse and say "I shall regain everything that I've lost"
"My revenge will be cruel I'll win at every cost".

"This is not the end but the beginning of my game,

He will come and remind me, My soul still the same,
Whole world will witness, The prince will rise again,
You all will remember Lord Averruncus Is The Name".

The Moon

When the night starts falling in the mist of sky,
I'll start glowing your world from above high,
You sleep tight keep dreaming in the mid night,
Burring all your fears so your dreams can rise.

My light will fade away the darkness within you
Some see my presence as lie and for some I'm true,
Even with the clouds surrounding, or it's the noon,
I'm always there shining, I'll always Be The Moon.

Your memories of me are black and white
Glaring up the sky in cold and lonely night
Winter and summer or the rain left and right
Silent wind dancing, slowly and bright.

When the time comes I will hide myself from you
It's the Eclipse for me but my light will come through
Even with the clouds surrounding, or it's the noon,
I'm always there Shining, I'll always be The Moon

Blossom In Veil

I've bloom again in the spirit of vain,
In the sun shower, I became a one little flower,
I might go to sleep when the night comes,
Until then I'm here, watching people go and come.

No one sees me, like I don't even exist,
I'm not a rose or a one Big tulip,
I'm also a flower, but without any scent,
It's a reality but we all fade away as the time went.

In the veil of time, He pass by the wind chime
Running through the valley, sighing on every sign,
Waiting for the moment, until he shall dwell,
The time will come, he'll be the Blossom In Veil.

I'm a flower that bloom again and again
Even if no one is around or it's the last rain
I'll bloom again in the spirit of vain.

The Demon From Hell 5 : Parade of Nightmare

Souls are trembling from fear, I'm having fun,
With over hundred thousand, an army of my demons,
Their face has no emotions, just the feel of numb,
Over my command, the night has finally come.

Sky is tearing apart, feel the meaning of fear,
I'm counting the numbers, how many dead are here ?
They are rising from the darkest place,
Face my demons, show your grace,
Revenge, Blood , your flesh we crave,
Prey the Gods, lord Averruncus waiting at your grave.

The Marching begins on the beat of the drum,
Now the countdown begins, three, two, one.
Empty streets filled with shadows of despair,
Your souls will scream, but who will care,
Stand against me, who will dare ?

My rules, my command, your fall is near,

You all shall perish, my goal is clear,
Your demise will be grand, hold on to what's so dear,
The final destination has arrived,
Welcome to the "Parade of Nightmare".

In Crimson Love The Cosmic Way

Starry nights, In my dreams you glow,
A Swift touch of wind, and your hairs blows,
Your rose hair pin shines like crimson red,
Can't take my eyes of you, this is really bad.

Oh my love, it's just my feelings for you,
I'm standing here, wish that you should've knew,
The first time our eyes met, it felt so nice,
Cosmic stars making the decision wise.

Aurora in your eyes always calming my soul,
Far from my reach, but my heart is being stole,
Unrequited love is too pain full to bear,
Watching you every day, just hoping you'll be near.

I'm in love that can't be Taken away,
Hoping you'll be mine, we hold our hands one day,
When the sky ignites and my poetry dance.
Violin playing the cosmic love romance.

I'm searching the reasons, so I can hate you,
But even cosmos saying, "error, your love is true",
Now I'm here having cosmic dreams of us all day,
I just want to know what is this ? I need you to say,
Cause I'm In Crimson Love The Cosmic Way.

River of Pain

I follow the sun to share some memories,
I believe in science and it's fellow theories,
I follow the truth and sometime cry,
I jump into the ocean of tears, which was dry,
I try to fight back, but I fell down again,
There is nothing in this life, except a river of pain.

Memories keep coming back, they becomes a infinite
loop,
Life keep drowning in problems, but we always group,
The time will teach us following the rhythm of life again,
Hope will rise, my fight won't be in vain
Even if I drown here again, even if it's a River of Pain.

Fading Memories

Slow and slow, when tears come again,
Flow and flow, when the wind blows in vain,
Cry and cry, when there is so much pain,
My Memories are fading my friend,
I need you to reset them.

Fly and fly, birds of freedom above high,
Chains crushing thier wings, they don't care just fly,
Blurry past keep covering with the thick fog,
I try to remember, but missing many dots,
Now the time is an amnesia, reaching its end,
My memories are fading my friend,
I need you to reset them.

My Moon Light The Sky

The moon I see, was always beyond me,
But it says to me, to shine so bright,
That everyone around you, can take your light,
In the world l lived, to the world I knew,
It was always them, but now it's you,
Take my light to glow your dreams,
I give you my shoulder come and lean
I guide you to home, I need you to stay.
Take my light before it fade away.

My way is clear, always towards you,
These emotions I hold, I must have knew
You are shining there Guiding me to light
I'm surrounded by love that shines so bright
May my way towards you will end soon
There will be a time,
when it's just be Me and My Moon.

Sea of Sorrow

I saw myself drowning in the sea of sorrow
Wanted to swim but it was too narrow ,

There was nothing that I can see
Just a little touch of a soft and cold breeze,

The Shore of hopes was far away
I tried to go but got betrayed,

The sea start sings to me in the rhythm of Hollow
again and again I got hit by the waves of Sorrow.

The 21

Under the gloomy sky, so many pages unfold,
Counting the miseries, some stories untold,
Some are the revivals, but many scars they hold,
Even if they're refined, pages will turn from new to old.

In the corner of shelf, dusty stories are settled
Books that says many Stories of warrior battles
Nostalgia of childhood is hitting in my veins
Memories that kept inside, will always remains.

21 are the Poems, eight Years in wisdom
I write with my heart, they are not my burden
Don't let them sit in dust, it's time to read again
21 are the Poems, don't let them go in vain.
Time will flow and stories and poems come to end
We all be gone one day and death becomes our friend.